THIS BOOK BELONGS

_____

_____

Seven Sabeels Press

السلام عليكم

Assalamualaikum,

May peace be upon you.

If you and your children enjoyed

this book and found it beneficial,

please help us to leave a review.

Thank you!

جزاك الله خير

Written by: Sheila Ibrahim

Illustrated by: Tony Surya

ISBN: 9798784079558

HOW TO DEAL WITH ANGER THE ISLAMIC WAY

"The strong man is not the one who can overpower others (in wrestling).
Rather, the strong man is the one who controls himself when he gets angry"

~ Prophet Muhammad (pbuh) ~

Sahih al-Bukhari 6114

One Sunday morning, Ali, the shortest kid in the neighborhood, was outside shooting hoops with his neighbors.

"Hey Shorty, I bet you can't block my shot!" teased Tommy, who lived opposite him.

Tommy aimed at the net and threw the ball. Although Ali jumped as high as he could, the ball went over his head and into the hoop. Everyone around him started to laugh.

Ali's face turned red with anger.

He clenched his fists and felt as if he was going to explode.

Without thinking, Ali marched over to Tommy and pushed him to the ground. "Ouch! My knee hurts!" cried Tommy. Ali's elder brother, Yusef, saw what happened and pulled Ali to the side.

"I can see why you're angry and it's okay to feel that way," said Yusef. "But it's never okay to hurt others. You must apologize."

Ali's heartbeat became faster and his breathing heavier.

Feeling angry and confused, he ran back into the house and up into his bedroom.

In the bedroom, Ali paced up and down. His palms were sweating. Just then, there was a knock on the door. "Ali, are you alright?" asked Yusef. Ali shook his head.

"Here, take a seat," said Yusef as he pulled out a chair.

Ali sat down and his breathing got easier. But still,

he could not shake off the anger in him.

"Our prophet, Muhammad, advised us to sit when we are angry and to lie down if the anger remains," Yusef added. "Why don't you lie down on the bed instead?"

After Yusef left the room, Ali lay on the bed with his hands by his side and closed his eyes. He could hear his breathing and feel his chest rising up and down. After a few minutes, his heart rate returned to normal and the anger in him disappeared.

A while later, Ali went down to the living room to watch television. He found his baby sister, Aisha, playing with his favorite fire truck toy, and one of the wheels had fallen off.

Suddenly, Ali felt his nostrils flaring. He snatched the toy truck

from Aisha which caused her to burst out in tears.

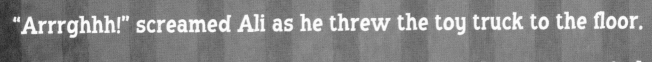

"Arrrghhh!" screamed Ali as he threw the toy truck to the floor.

"*Astaghfirullah*," gasped Ali's mother. "Son, whenever you feel
angry, say: *A'udhu billahi minash shaytanir rajim* ."

أَعُوْذُ بِاللهِ مِنَ الشَّيْطَانِ الرَّجِيْم

Usually, Ali would simply sulk in anger. But there was something in those words that soothed his heart. Ali took a deep breath and slowly repeat the phrase aloud.

أَعُوْذُ بِاللّٰهِ مِنَ الشَّيْطَانِ الرَّجِيْم

"That's right, my dear. It means, 'I seek refuge with Allah from the cursed Satan,'" explained Ali's mother. The thought of *Shaytan* being so far away made Ali feel so much calmer.

Later that afternoon, the family gathered at the dining table.

But before Ali could take a bite of his lunch, his father said,

"Ali, you have to apologize to Tommy."

The thought of Tommy teasing him caused

Ali's ears to turn red. "No way!" roared Ali as

he stomped his feet.

"Son, you look as if there's a fire within you,"

said Ali's father. "You know what? Let's go

take *wudu*."

"Our prophet, Muhammad, advised us to take *wudu* when we are angry," Ali's father explained. "The water will put out the fire in us. *SubhanAllah!*"

As Ali performed his *wudu*, he imagined his fire truck toy spraying water at him on a hot summer day. When he was done, Ali felt refreshed, and his mind became clearer too.

"A'udhu billahi minash shaytanir rajim." said Ali aloud.

" *Masha Allah!* That's exactly how our prophet, Muhammad,

would choose to react if he was angry," said Ali's mother.

"He was always slow to anger and quick to forgive."

Ali remained silent. Deep down, he wanted to be like the Prophet.

"Tommy hurt my feelings, but I forgive him," announced Ali. "It was also wrong of me to lose my temper. I shouldn't have hurt Tommy, throw my toy truck, or raise my voice. I will apologize to Tommy, and I hope he will forgive me too."

" *Alhamdullilah!* I'm so proud of you for following the *sunnah*," said Ali's father.

As Ali walked over to Tommy's house, he felt light as a feather. He was no longer feeling angry. But above all, Ali was glad that he had learned how to deal with his anger, the Islamic way.

The End

"A moment of patience in a moment of anger prevents a thousand moments of regret."

~ Ali Ibn Abi Talib ~

GLOSSARY

- ## Astaghfirullah

This word means "I seek forgiveness from Allah," and we usually say it when we had done or witnessed a wrong or shameful act.

- ## A'udhu billahi minash shaytanir rajim

This phrase means "I seek refuge with Allah from the cursed Satan". We recite this to ask Allah to protect us from the devil and his evil whisperings. The phrase is usually continued with "Bismillahir rahmanir rahim".

- ## Wudu

Wudu refers to the ritual washing of parts of the body to cleanse ourselves before performing acts of worship.

- ## SubhanAllah

This word is commonly translated as "Glory be to Allah," and it refers to the perfection of Allah who is free from any defects. We usually say it when we are amazed by His wonderful creations and want to praise Him.

- **Masha Allah**

This word means "As what Allah has willed," and we usually say it to express our amazement towards someone or for something that happened. We also say it to express our appreciation towards Allah since all things can only be achieved by His will.

- **Alhamdullilah**

This word means "All praise and thanks be to Allah." We say it when we want to express our gratitude and thank Allah for His blessings.

- **Shaytan**

Shaytan is our invisible enemy whose job is to encourage us to commit sin and evil deeds, and to stray away from the right path.

- **Sunnah**

Sunnah refers to the way Prophet Muhammad lived his life. It includes his practices, actions, and sayings. The sunnah is an excellent model which Muslims should strive to follow in order to please Allah.

SUMMARY

In Islam, there are several recommended ways to deal with anger. The following are the most common ways to do so which are supported by authentic hadiths (a narrative record of the Prophet's sayings and traditions).

1) Changing our positions

- Prophet Muhammad once said, "If any of you becomes angry and he is standing, let him sit down so his anger will go away. Otherwise, let him lie down."
- Reported by Abu Dharr. Source: Sunan Abu Dawud 4782

2) Reciting "A'udhu billahi minash shaytanir rajim"

- Once, there were two men arguing and one of them had gotten so furious that his face turned red with anger. Prophet Muhammad remarked that if one were to say "A'udhu billahi minash shaytanir rajim", his rage would go away. That means 'I seek refuge with Allah from the cursed Satan'.
- Narrated by Sulaiman bin Surad. Source: Sahih al-Bukhari 3282

3) Taking wudu

- Prophet Muhammad once said, "Anger comes from Satan and Satan was created from fire. Fire is extinguished with water, so if you become angry then perform ablution with water."
- Narrated by Atiyyah as-Sa'di. Source: Sunan Abu Dawud 4784

Another way to deal with anger is to take slow and deep breaths. Focusing on your breathing will help to take your mind off the anger as you cool yourself down. You can do this while sitting or lying down.

Anger is one of the emotions that human beings universally experience. However, we have the power to choose how to react in moments of anger. If we don't learn how to control our temper, we might do things that would be undesirable which we would regret later.

InshaAllah (God Willing), if we follow the sunnah on how to deal with anger, we should be able to avoid such regret and negative consequences. Following the sunnah would also make Allah pleased with us, and He would reward us accordingly.

OTHER BOOKS BY SEVEN SABEELS PRESS

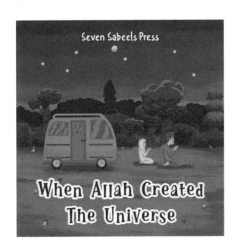

**Let's Learn More About
Eid al-Adha**

**When Allah Created
The Universe**

If you and your children enjoyed
this book and found it beneficial,
please help us to leave a review.
Thank you!

جزاك الله خير

Made in the USA
Las Vegas, NV
01 February 2024

85191843R00021